TOW TRUCKS

by Mary Winget
and W. Bryan Winget

Lerner Publications Company • Minneapolis

For Tiernan and his great grandpa

Text copyright © 2007 by Lerner Publications Company

All rights reserved. International copyright secured. No part of this book may be reproduced, stored in a retrieval system, or transmitted in any form or by any means—electronic, mechanical, photocopying, recording, or otherwise—without the prior written permission of Lerner Publishing Group, except for the inclusion of brief quotations in an acknowledged review.

Lerner Publications Company
A division of Lerner Publishing Group
241 First Avenue North
Minneapolis, MN 55401 U.S.A.

Website address: www.lernerbooks.com

Words in **bold type** are explained in a glossary on page 30.

Library of Congress Cataloging-in-Publication Data

Winget, Mary.
     Tow trucks / by Mary Winget and W. Bryan Winget.
          p.   cm. — (Pull ahead books)
     Includes index.
     ISBN-13: 978-0-8225-6006-7 (lib. bdg. : alk. paper)
     ISBN-10: 0-8225-6006-2 (lib. bdg. : alk. paper)
     1. Wreckers (Vehicles)—Juvenile literature.
2. Automobiles—Towing—Juvenile literature. I. Winget, W.
Bryan. II. Title. III. Series.
TL230.5.W74W56 2007
629.225—dc22   2005024183

Manufactured in the United States of America
1 2 3 4 5 6 — JR — 12 11 10 09 08 07

Look at the bright flashing lights on that truck! What kind of truck is it?

This is a tow truck. Flashing lights tell people that a tow truck is at work.

What do tow trucks do?

Tow trucks go to **emergencies**. They are called when cars need help.

Who drives tow trucks to emergencies?
Tow truck drivers do. The drivers sit in
the **cab**.

They push buttons in the cab. The buttons turn the tow trucks' lights on or off.

Tow truck drivers use tools to help in emergencies. This tow truck driver is changing a flat tire.

Tow trucks carry lots of tools. Where are all the tools kept?

Doors on the outside of the tow truck open. Tools are stored behind them.

This driver has locked her keys in her car. How will she get the doors unlocked?

Tow trucks
have tools to
unlock cars.
A **slim jim**
slides between
the window
and the door.
It unlocks
the door.

This car won't start. It has no power.
Cars need power to make them start.

Jumper cables help give power to the car. Then the car can start.

Cars that are wrecked or won't work
need to be towed.

Tow trucks have special **equipment** for towing.

There are levers on the back of the truck. Each lever works a different part of the tow truck.

One of the levers moves the **wheel lift**.
The wheel lift lowers to the ground.

The wheel lift fits around the car's front wheels.

The tow truck driver pushes another
lever. The wheel lift picks up the front
of the car.

Wheel straps hold the wheels in place.
This car is ready to be towed.

Oh no! This car slid off the road. How will it get out of the ditch?

A tow truck will pull it out with a **winch**.

A winch has a long, strong wire.
The wire connects to the car.

The winch pulls the car out of
the ditch.

Sometimes big trucks and buses need help too. Is this truck too big for a tow truck to help?

No. Giant tow trucks can tow big trucks and buses. Tow trucks can help any car in trouble.

Fun Facts about Tow Trucks

- Ernest W. Holmes Sr. made the first tow truck in 1916. He bolted three poles on the frame of a 1913 Cadillac. Then he attached a pulley with a hand-operated winch to the poles. Finally, he added a chain to hang off the back.

- Many years ago, tow trucks were also traveling service stations. They carried tires and tools to broken cars. The cars got fixed on the side of the road. If they couldn't be fixed, they were towed to a repair shop.

- Most people call tow trucks to start car engines on cold mornings, change tires, or open locked car doors.

- Tow trucks called flatbeds can tow two cars at the same time. At airports, tow trucks even pull airplanes!

Parts of a Tow Truck

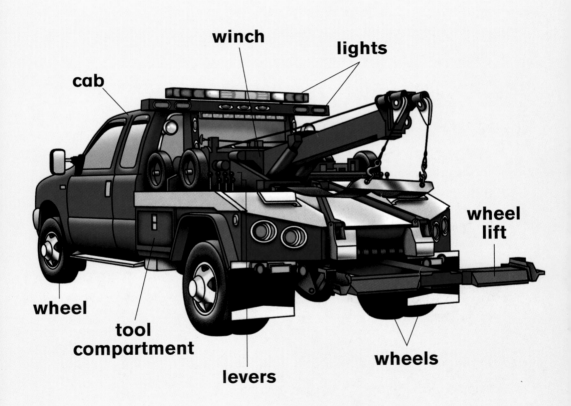

winch

lights

cab

wheel lift

wheel

tool compartment

levers

wheels

Glossary

cab: the part of a tow truck where the driver sits

emergencies: serious problems that need help quickly

equipment: parts of a tow truck that are used to help cars in trouble

jumper cables: special wires used to help start cars

slim jim: a long, flat tool used to unlock car doors

wheel lift: a part that lifts one end of a car by the wheels

winch: a powerful machine used for pulling things

More about Tow Trucks

Check out these books and websites to find out more about tow trucks.

Books

Graham, Ian. *Super Trucks.* New York: Franklin Watts, 2001.
   Full-color illustrations give readers a behind-the-scenes look
   at how big trucks work.

Oxlade, Chris. *Emergency Vehicles.* Chicago: Heinemann
   Library, 2001.
   This book describes different forms of emergency vehicles and
   how they are used around the world.

Pomerantz, Charlotte. *How Many Trucks Can a Tow Truck Tow?*
   New York: Random House, 1987.
   Read this fun story of a tow truck that rescues other tow trucks.

Websites

Car Corner: Professor Speaks
   http://www.chevroncars.com/wocc/lrn/artcl/artcl.jhtml?id=/
   content/Car_Corner/a0421.xml
   Professor Trevor Tow Truck talks about the first tow trucks.

Kids' Korner
   http://www.millerind.com/english/kids/index.html
   Color Tommy the Towtruck and his friends, or play online
   games such as Tic-Tac-Towing and Match-A-Tration.

Index

Photo Acknowledgments

The photographs in this book appear with the permission of: © Sam Lund/Independent Picture Service, front cover, pp. 7, 8, 9, 10, 16, 17, 19, 20, 25; © 2006 W. Bryan Winget, pp. 3, 23; © Alan Schein Photography/CORBIS, p. 4; © Jim Reed/CORBIS, p. 5; © Todd Strand/Independent Picture Service, pp. 6, 12, 14, 18, 21, 24; © David Woods/CORBIS, p. 11; © age fotostock/SuperStock, p. 13; © Gail Mooney/CORBIS, p. 15; © AP/Wide World Photos, pp. 22, 26; © Gunter Marx Photography/CORBIS, p. 27. Illustration on p. 29 by © Laura Westlund/Independent Picture Service.